A Comprehensive Guide to Amazon Prime

and The Kindle Owners' Lending Library

Disclaimer

All information, ideas, and guidelines presented here are only for educational purposes.

While the author has taken utmost efforts to ensure the accuracy of the written content, all readers are advised to follow information mentioned herein at their own risk. The author cannot be held responsible for any personal or commercial damage caused by misinterpretation of information. All readers are encouraged to seek professional advice when needed.

What Will You Get From This eBook?

If you are interested in Amazon Prime membership but are not sure about its services and benefits, then this eBook can serve as the perfect guidance source for you. Also, if you crave for the latest and classic books but have no idea about the working of Kindle Owners' Lending Library, then you should definitely read this helpful guide.

Want to know more about the major highlights of Amazon Prime membership? This eBook offers complete information about Amazon Prime and its various beneficial services. This guide will provide you confidence and knowledge you need to avail valuable features of Amazon Prime.

Table of Contents

Amazon Prime – A Brief Overview

Amazon Prime is an extraordinary membership service that was first introduced in the year 2005 by Amazon.com. Initially released in the United States, this exclusive service amazed the entire world and made a great impression on people belonging to different classes. Since then, it has become a critical necessity for individuals. This might be the reason why you want to become an Amazon Prime member immediately. More benefits and features of Amazon Prime membership are coming up later, but don't forget to take your Kindle Fire HD out to enter the world of Amazon.com.

Amazon.com didn't take much time to introduce the services of Amazon Prime in Germany, Japan, France, and the United Kingdom. The primary highlights of Amazon Prime include free shipping services, video streaming, and the Kindle Owners' Lending Library.

The offerings of Amazon Prime are particularly beneficial for people who make online purchases, watch online content, or are book lovers. Since its services are available at minimal rates, people are able to enjoy great features while making substantial savings.

Kindle Fire HD is a great device that offers superb features to its users. This is the reason why people can't wait to become a member of Amazon Prime and avail its tremendous benefits.

The main offerings of Amazon Prime membership include:

1. Free shipping of all your purchases within two days.
2. Instant video streaming.
3. Access to unlimited books of the Kindle Owners' Lending Library.

What's more, you don't have to pay anything for these services for the period of thirty days. This is definitely great news as you can make the most of your Kindle Fire HD without worrying about expenses.

Shipping services of Amazon Prime are not only affordable, but are also convenient and quick. This service gives you absolute peace of mind with the idea that all your items and products are delivered at your doorstep for free. Moreover, it doesn't test your patience as your purchases are shipped safely within 2 days.

Amazon Prime has facilitated people in different ways. It has become one of the most reliable and affordable sources to purchase varied household items, including toiletries, cleaning products, or groceries, that most people need on regular basis. Most of all, you can enjoy great discounts for each purchase you make via Amazon Prime.

Have a Free Trial

If you are not sure about Amazon Prime's paid membership, then become its free trial member as it will give you a clear idea about its features and offerings. Though Amazon Prime gives equal importance to its free trial members and paid members, the latter ones are able to enjoy even greater benefits.

If you want to become a free trial member, just visit the Amazon Prime's sign-up page to get a free 30-day trial. At the end of your trial period, you'll certainly get hopelessly addicted to impeccable services of Amazon Prime. Considering your liking, Amazon Prime will give you an option to become a permanent member and enjoy unlimited benefits.

Start Your 30-Day Free Trial

Are You Eligible? Know the Conditions

If you want to avail a free trial option of Amazon Prime, then go through the following terms and conditions to determine if you are eligible to become its free member:

1. You should own a current and working credit card. Amazon Prime does not allow its free trial members to pay for their purchases via particular payment options, such as checking accounts or gift cards.

2. Being a free trial member, you won't have to pay for any Amazon Prime services. Nevertheless, as soon as your free trial membership ends, it will automatically be changed into paid membership.

3. Amazon.com is fully authorized to make a final decision regarding your eligibility for free trial membership. Your membership history plays a vital role in this decision.

Can You Get Free Trial Benefits?

Amazon Prime provides great facilities and services to its free trial members. Being a trial member, you can easily get all valuable features that a paid member avails. Moreover, you have an authority to request Amazon Prime not to automatically convert your free membership into paid membership.

After becoming a free trial member of Amazon Prime, you can adjust your ordering settings at any time according to your preferences and needs. Furthermore, you can easily share your free membership benefits with your family members.

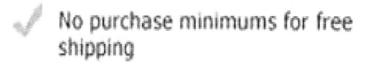

Get Amazon Prime Membership

As soon as your 30-day free trial period ends, Amazon Prime automatically updates your free membership to the paid one. As a paid member, you'll have to pay yearly charges to enjoy exceptional services of Amazon Prime.

If you are not interested in paid membership of Amazon Prime, then you can opt out of this offer by changing your account settings during the trial period.

Can You Get Membership Benefits?

If you've decided to become a paid member of Amazon Prime, then you should know several benefits that it can offer. In addition to providing you with various shipping options, it allows you to get all your eligible purchases right at your doorstep within two days. Above all, you get your items without making any extra payments.

Amazon Prime members enjoy:

Free Two-Day Shipping + Instant streaming of movies & TV shows + Instant access to Kindle Books

Amazon Prime also allows its paid members to enjoy valuable services like Amazon Instant Video. With this service, you can purchase or rent television shows, videos, or movies present in the online library of Amazon. As an added bonus, you get a chance to access unlimited books from the Kindle Owners' Lending Library.

Reliable Services at Affordable Rates

Being a paid member of Amazon Prime, you can make the most of its shipping services. To get these services, you have to pay minimal yearly charges. Simply pay $79 per year to get all your items that you purchase via Amazon. You'll definitely find this shipping service quite reasonable as it doesn't disturb your savings and finances. Above all, you get a rare opportunity to enjoy a myriad of convenient and valuable services at affordable rates.

Can You Share Your Membership Benefits?

Amazon Prime allows paid as well as free members to share their shipping services with whoever they want. So go ahead and share your shipping benefits with up to four individuals, either friends or family members. Nevertheless, you may not be able to share other services, including Amazon Prime Instant Video and the Kindle Owners' Lending Library, with anyone else.

Remember to verify your membership particulars before you invite others to share your membership benefits. You cannot share your membership benefits with a person who is already a member of Amazon Students or Amazon Mom.

Is Amazon Prime Available For You?

Amazon Prime allows everyone to enjoy its standard services and offerings. Nevertheless, its streaming video features are only available for people in the United States.

On the other hand, you can use free 2-day shipping services for all products that you purchase via Amazon. Your purchases will get standard shipping if they are considered as huge, risky, or heavy items. This means that you'll receive your items in about five to eight days. All your products that need to be delivered to P.O. boxes with U.S. zip codes follow the same rules defined for standard shipping.

Getting Membership – Is It the Right Choice?

Becoming a paid member of Amazon Prime is your own decision that should be based on your individual needs and preferences. Analyze your requirements before you choose to convert your free membership into the paid one. Getting Amazon Prime membership is definitely a brilliant idea if you make frequent online purchases. Nothing can be better than getting all your items and products right at your home without paying any additional charges.

Furthermore, if you constantly look for something fun and entertaining, then Amazon Prime Instant Videos is just the service for you. Streaming videos, television content, or movies; this service provides you with unlimited options so as to ensure that nothing stays out of your reach. On comparing subscription charges of standard streaming websites with that of Amazon Prime membership, you'll realize that Amazon Prime allows you to enjoy unlimited content for a dime.

Instant streaming of
movies & TV shows

If you are an ardent fan of classic books and renowned authors, then you shouldn't miss the opportunity of enjoying features of the Kindle Owners' Lending Library. It allows you to access millions of extraordinary books that you may not find anywhere else.

Instant access to
Kindle Books

What Will You Get From Amazon Prime Membership?

Amazon Prime provides the following benefits, services, and offerings to its paid members:

1. Free delivery of all items and products that a member purchases via Amazon in two days.

2. Amazon Prime does not restrict its members by minimum prices or purchasable items.

3. A member is allowed to watch movies, streaming videos, and television shows.

4. A member is allowed to borrow countless books from the Kindle Owners' Lending Library.

Receive Your Purchases via Free Shipping Services

All Amazon Prime members can avail free shipping benefits. If you have become a paid member, then your orders and products will be delivered within two days without you having to make additional payments. On the other hand, if you are not a Prime member, then in addition to paying additional charges, you'll have to wait for 4 to 5 days to receive your items.

Free Two-Day
Shipping

Shipping charges usually vary according to the items you order and the region you live in. You may have to pay hefty amounts for simple purchases, such as a few CDs, books, and other household products. On the other hand, shipping services of Amazon Prime are quite reasonable and affordable.

Watch Unlimited Content via Instant Videos

The Instant Video feature of Amazon Prime enables all members to watch their favorite television shows, classic movies, and extraordinary videos. To enjoy this service, they are allowed to use any of their high-tech gadgets and devices as long as they can be connected to the Internet.

Amazon.com updates its video catalog regularly. Since Amazon signs license agreements with different studios, it may present some movies and shows for a limited period. This is hardly a noticeable downside as your membership allows you to watch whatever you want.

Read Countless Books via Kindle Owners' Lending Library

Though a virtual library, the Kindle Owners' Lending Library has effectively replaced any physical library. It has the perfect offerings and services to cater to diverse reading needs and choices. Its offerings include loads of categories, unlimited books, and lots of authors. It never leaves you disappointed and gives you a chance to get your hands on your favorite book written by the author you enjoy the most.

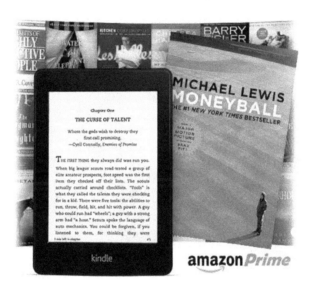

Perks You Should Know About

1. No matter if you are a movie fan or a book lover, Amazon Prime keeps you entertained at all times.

2. You are allowed to share your membership benefits with four other individuals. This further brings down individual charges per person.

3. Despite offering economical services, Amazon Prime ensures huge benefits.

4. You get a chance to watch as many movies and videos as you like.

5. The Kindle Owners' Lending Library contains innumerable interesting reads.

6. It is pretty simple to watch movie and borrow books from Amazon Prime.

7. You can get these extraordinary benefits for free for an entire month.

Some Other Particulars

1. The Instant Video feature of Amazon Prime is available only for U.S. residents.

2. You are allowed to borrow one book at a time.

What is Kindle Owners' Lending Library?

If you have Amazon Prime membership, then feel free to enjoy the offerings of the Kindle Owners' Lending Library. Using this service, you can read as many books as you want on your Kindle Fire HD without paying any additional charges. The library currently offers almost 300,000 books that you can borrow for free. Furthermore, you can continue reading a book for as long as you want.

You can't use your iPad, iPhone, or Android device to read this virtual library's books. It is possible to download, borrow, and read a book multiple times. If you decide to opt out of paid membership, then Amazon Prime will not allow you to avail its free download services.

Kindle Owners' Lending Library

Supported Devices and Gadgets

All Kindle devices support the Kindle Owners' Lending Library. You can enjoy this service via Kindle Touch, Kindle Fire tablet, Kindle 4, Kindle Keyboard, and other Kindle e-readers. But your standard iPad and iPhone don't support the KOLL. Furthermore, you cannot check out the shelves of this virtual library via your iOS, Android, Desktop, or webOS.

Working of Kindle Owners' Lending Library

Amazon Prime allows its members to borrow a book every month from the Kindle Owners' Lending Library. You can download and read a book on any of your Kindle devices. You are allowed to keep your books for as long as you want, but it is possible to borrow only one book at a time. If you already have a book and try to borrow another one, the previous book will automatically be removed from your device. If you buy or borrow the same book again, it will automatically have all your previous bookmarks, highlights, notes, and annotations.

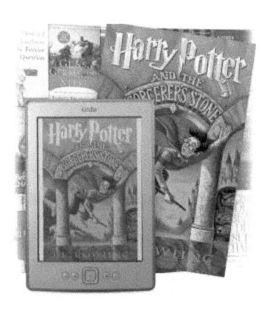

Are You Eligible for the KOLL?

Though the features and offerings of the Kindle Owners' Lending Library are great to use, it requires you to fulfill certain conditions. You can enjoy Amazon's Instant Video on several devices and gadgets, but the KOLL does not provide you with that freedom. In order to access this virtual library, you need to own either Kindle Fire or Kindle eReader.

Additionally, Amazon Prime membership is another prerequisite if you wish to borrow books from the KOLL. Currently, only the paid members of Amazon Prime can avail this great service. This implies that you must become a paid member of Amazon Prime to relish superb features of this virtual library.

Why You Should Choose the KOLL

1. You don't have to pay any extra charges to borrow the latest and famous eBooks.

2. The Kindle Owners' Lending Library does not involve waiting lists or limited prints.

3. There are no due dates.

4. It consists of several New York Best Sellers and rare books.

5. You are allowed to make notes and bookmarks in your eBook. You can even highlight the text.

Books and Publishers

Though some reputed publishers of the United States are not presently working with the Kindle Owners' Lending Library, the offerings of this amazing lending service include countless popular classics, informational books, and how-to books.

     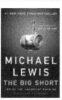

    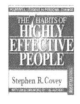

Know the Rules

You have to follow a pretty simple process to borrow or purchase eBooks from the Kindle Owners' Lending Library. It involves a few basic rules, mentioned as follows:

1. You are allowed to borrow only one book a month.

2. You are allowed to borrow only one book at a time. It is necessary to return the previous book before getting another one.

3. You are allowed to read a particular book on multiple Kindle devices as long as all devices are registered under your Prime account.

4. You are not allowed to share your borrowed book with any other user.

Get the Most Exclusive Books

Being an Amazon Prime member, you can enjoy a multitude of classic and outstanding books published by reputable brands and written by renowned authors. For ardent fans of classics, the KOLL offers great literary works like Treasure Island by Robert Louis Stevenson and Alice in Wonderland by Lewis Carroll. On the other hand, it comprises of some recently published books such as Fuse of Armageddon by Hank Hanegraaff and Sigmund Brouwer and The Hunger Games trilogy by Suzanne Collins as well.

The following list mentions only a few offerings of the Kindle Owners' Lending Library:

1. The God Delusion by Richard Dawkins.

2. Water for Elephants by Sara Gruen.

3. Innocent Little Crimes by C.S Lakin.

4. Cult of Beauty: The Secret Life of a Supermodel by K M Dylan.

5. Dangerous Affairs by Diana Miller.

6. Concrete Pearl by Vincent Zandri.

7. Beyond the Sand Creek Bridge by Scott Wyatt.

8. Pharaoh's Son by Diana Wilder.

9. Portrait of a Gossip by Melanie Jackson.

10. Mockingjay by Suzanne Collins.

11. Clutching at Straws by J.L. Abramo.

12. Punctured by Rex Kusler.

13. Castle Cay by Lee Hanson.

14. Missed by Lisa Bork.

15. Liar's Poker by Michael Lewis.

16. The Puzzle by Peggy A. Edelheit.

17. Persephone Cole and the Halloween Curse by Heather Haven.

18. My Name is Joe by Stefan Bourque.

19. Moneyball: The Art of Winning an Unfair Game by Michael Lewis.

20. Section 132 by Helga Zeiner

How to Borrow Books?

Being an eligible member of Amazon Prime, you can borrow and read innumerable eBooks from the Kindle Owners' Lending Library. The most amazing thing of the KOLL is that you never have to worry about due dates while borrowing eBooks from this virtual library.

If you own a Kindle Fire HD, then you have to follow a certain procedure to borrow a book from the Kindle Owners' Lending Library:

1. Use your Kindle Fire HD to search through the Kindle Fire store. It will provide you with different categories. Select the Kindle Owners' Lending Library to borrow a free book.

2. Select a book having the "Prime" sign. This symbol indicates that a book is available to be borrowed.

3. You can either borrow or purchase a book. Choose the "Borrow" option to have the eBook on your Kindle Fire HD for as long as you want.

How to Read Books?

You can use any Kindle device to read your favorite book borrowed from the Kindle Owners' Lending Library. Nevertheless, it is necessary to use a Kindle device that is registered under your Amazon Prime account. Additionally, it is not possible to use any Kindle reading application for eBooks of the Kindle Owners' Lending Library.

Though you are allowed to borrow only one book per month, you can continue reading it for as long as you like.

How to Return Books?

The Kindle Owners' Lending Library does not allow its users to borrow more than one book at a time. It is necessary to return the previous book before getting another one. You are allowed to modify your Amazon Prime account settings to handle book returns more efficiently.

Kindle Fire HD – A Perfect Means to Improve Your Reading Experience

Besides enhancing your reading experience, stunning display screen of Kindle Fire HD allows you to enjoy exciting music, amazing applications, thrilling movies, and fun games. In addition to having a rich and bright display, the sophisticated stereo speakers of Kindle Fire HD enable you to experience the most awe-inspiring sound effects.

If you want to enjoy high-quality text of your eBooks, then Kindle Fire HD can prove to be the best choice. Having an enhanced display screen, it makes the text real, easy-to-read, and more enjoyable.

Time to Try Astounding Amazon Services

The availability of user-friendly and convenient Kindle devices has facilitated individuals to browse, borrow, download, read, and buy books, newspapers, blogs, magazines, and other literary works via Amazon. You can select your favorite device from varied Kindle eBook readers to enjoy the amazing services of Amazon's Kindle Owners' Lending Library.

Amazon Prime enables you to try its amazing services for an entire month without paying any additional charges. By the end of this free trial period, you'll definitely fall in love with its various services and pay yearly charges to enjoy amazing membership benefits.

www.ingramcontent.com/pod-product-compliance
Lightning Source LLC
Chambersburg PA
CBHW060514060326
40689CB00020B/4739